T0161570

# LEAD

THE

# FIELD

**FOR FINANCIAL PROFESSIONALS**

# LEAD
### THE
# FIELD

**FOR FINANCIAL PROFESSIONALS**

HOW TO

**BECOME AN AUTHORITY** AND

**DOMINATE YOUR COMPETITION**

# HARPER TUCKER
# ADAM WITTY

**Forbes**Books

Published by ForbesBooks, Charleston, South Carolina.
Member of Advantage Media Group.

ForbesBooks is a registered trademark, and the ForbesBooks colophon is a trademark of Forbes Media, LLC.

Printed in the United States of America.

10   9   8   7   6   5   4   3   2   1

ISBN: 978-1-946633-24-8
LCCN: 2017954146

Cover and layout design by George Stevens.

This publication is designed to provide accurate and authoritative information in regard to the subject matter covered. It is sold with the understanding that the publisher is not engaged in rendering legal, accounting, or other professional services. If legal advice or other expert assistance is required, the services of a competent professional person should be sought.

ForbesBooks is proud to be a part of the Tree Neutral® program. Tree Neutral offsets the number of trees consumed in the production and printing of this book by taking proactive steps such as planting trees in direct proportion to the number of trees used to print books. To learn more about Tree Neutral, please visit **www.treeneutral.com.**

Since 1917, the Forbes mission has remained constant. Global Champions of Entrepreneurial Capitalism. ForbesBooks exists to further that aim by bringing the Stories, Passion, and Knowledge of top thought leaders to the forefront. ForbesBooks brings you The Best in Business. To be considered for publication, please visit **www.forbesbooks.com.**

This book is dedicated to all of the real estate, law, and financial professionals that have Stories, Passion, and Knowledge to share with the world.

# TABLE OF CONTENTS

# THE POWER OF AUTHORITY

by Dan Kennedy

America's #1 Marketing Advisor,
Author of over 20 best-selling marketing books

**dankennedy.com**
**nobsbooks.com**

There is a huge secret about income that only a small percentage of top earners in every field ever figure out and use to their advantage. Most others are ignorant of it, but some see it, and instead of using it, they deeply and bitterly resent it. The secret is that *the higher up in income you go, in almost any category, the more you are paid for who you are rather than for what you do*. That often isn't just, in the way that most people think about justice, and I can't attempt to affect how you think about this in the few words I have for the introduction to this book, so for now I'll simply state it as the bald fact that it is.

The number-one key to making yourself a powerful, magnetic, trusted, high-income "who" to any target audience or market is your known and accepted status as an authority.

## BE SEEN AS THE AUTHORITY, NOT THE SALESPERSON

If you are wandering about in the forest, you will probably recognize a bear if you encounter one. You know bears are big, furry, black, or brown, with snouts, and so on. You've seen photos. You've seen them on TV and in movies.

Similarly, you know how to spot a dreaded salesperson in the woods. He has lots of brochures, maybe a PowerPoint presentation on a laptop, and other sales matter. He usually assaults you and tries to get you to an appointment by various stratagems. In his cubicle or office, there are plaques and trophies proclaiming his sales prowess. Like bears, these sales creatures are to be feared and avoided.

Although I have been a salesman virtually every day of my life, I have gone to great pains not to be perceived as one. Beginning very early in my career to the present, I have implemented an overall marketing strategy to elevate my authority in the minds of my clientele so that I am not perceived as a salesman. Rather, my business comes to me because *money follows and flows to authority.*

For me, the journey toward this authority status began when I first published *The Ultimate Sales Letter* in 1981—a book that has been on bookstore shelves without interruption ever since. It established me as an expert in the craftsmanship of letters that sell. It directly brought me clients, but much more importantly, it elevated my status above other copywriters. People wanted to hear from and get assistance from "the guy who wrote the book" about sales letters, and it is not accidental that the preemptive word "the" is in that title.

I have since written more than thirty books with seven different publishing companies and have gone to considerable effort to effectively implement an ongoing marketing strategy around them, keeping them in print and distribution and using the authority conveyed by being the author of each book and of an entire series of books to every possible advantage.

Back when I flew commercial—I now travel by private jet—and when I was still on the hunt for clients and business, I always had copies of my books in my carry-on. In 1985, I was in first-class, on a flight from Phoenix to Houston, and the fellow next to me struck up the usual conversation. He identified himself as owner of a Houston-based advertising agency and asked what I did. Instead of an answer or "elevator speech," I stood up, got a copy of *The Ultimate Sales Letter* book, handed it to him, and excused myself for a trip to the bathroom. Two weeks later, I was conducting a nicely compensated training session for his staff copywriters, where he proudly told them, "Today, I have brought you the man who wrote the book on sales letter writing."

One more story about that first book: the owner of a very large, fast-growing weight-loss company with a hot celebrity endorser, a robust direct-marketing campaign, and distribution in Wal-Mart brought me to his company headquarters to spend a day discussing direct marketing with his entire staff, followed by a second day working with his three copywriters.

At the start of the first day, he told me he had given *The Ultimate Sales Letter* to everybody a week before so that they would be prepared. He then asked if everybody had read it and announced he was going to conduct a quick, impromptu quiz on the book before I got started. One guy sheepishly admitted he'd been too busy to read the book. My client instantly fired him.

He said, "I've invested in bringing the number-one expert in this field in. If you couldn't invest an hour or two preparing, I do not wish to continue investing in you."

Clients acquire status by having a leading expert working for them. Typically, when prospective clients come to me as a referral, they report that the referring client either told them about one of my books and urged them to get it and read it or gifted them one of my books.

This is what I call the "expert status halo." People are proud of their association with an expert, be that the number-one expert on home decorating in Abilene or the number-one expert on direct-response marketing and copywriting in the world (me).

## MUST YOU SELL OR CAN YOU PRESCRIBE?

Certain experts, professionals, and providers do not sell their recommendations; they have the authority needed to prescribe.

Authority comes from a matrix of factors, including expert status as well as environment, mind-set of customer, criticality of solution, and others. If you have a stomachache that won't go away and hustle over to the local "doc-in-a-box" urgent-care clinic, you'll probably fill a prescription he issues without question, but you probably wouldn't let him cut you open and remove an organ without a lot of questions; you would demand a second opinion.

However, if your chronic stomach pain takes you from your MD to a specialist at the Cleveland Clinic, who brings in another specialist, and they prescribe urgent surgery, you most likely will sign the form, lie down on the steel cart, and be wheeled away without checking out information via Google.

The solution proposed is the same in both scenarios. *The difference in your reaction is entirely based on your acceptance of the authority of the person making the recommendation.*

In my own consulting and copywriting practice, I often present complex projects that involve fees from $75,000 to $200,000, plus royalties, and are often more complex and require more investment than a new client has prepared himself for. I never want to have to sell such a thing. I have developed a thorough, carefully choreographed process to avoid having to sell my service.

The following is a brief overview: A potential client typically comes forward from my books, from a referral, from participating in a seminar, or from within Glazer-Kennedy Insider's Circle (GKIC) membership. The potential client is prevented from contacting me via phone or otherwise and instead is required to fax me a memo describing his business and perceived needs. He first receives a written reply, usually accompanied by one or several of my books. He must then take the initiative to book a consulting day, positioned as "diagnostic and prescriptive" (at my base fee of $18,800).

He may be told of or sent a book of mine to read. He has to travel to me for the day. Before day's end, he is asking me to issue a prescription—which I do. And nine out of ten times it is accepted. This is the power of authority.

Great GKIC members in a very different field, Jeff Giagnocavo and Ben McClure, are authors of *What's Keeping You Up at Night?* and owners of Gardner's Mattress, where their mattresses are priced from $4,000 to $35,000, even while encircled by mattress stores selling at or below the national average of $700.

I am impressed by and very proud of these guys. Everybody else sells mattresses. They prescribe.

In the store, the customer is engaged in a diagnostic conversation. For many, a particular mattress is then prescribed and taken from the showroom floor into the private Dream Room®, a room that mimics a luxury hotel suite, where the customer and spouse spend one, two, or even three hours—

they are able to nap, watch TV, read, and fully, comfortably experience the chosen bed.

To date, the percentage of customers who buy after trying out the bed in the Dream Room® is— drum roll, please—100 percent.

This is the power of authority.

One of the GKIC members in my top coaching program is Steve Adams, the owner of twenty-one exceptionally profitable retail pet stores. In each store, there is a professional pet nutrition counselor who engages customers in a diagnostic process to then prescribe the best customized diet and food for that person's pet. The total customer value and retention is much, much higher than ordinary stores manage.

That's the power of authority.

If you want to be liberated from selling, if you want to prescribe rather than sell, then you need to focus on building your status, building your authority, and becoming the leader in your field.

## THE IRRATIONAL REACTION TO STAR POWER

As I am writing this, there are two supremely successful TV ad campaigns you have probably seen *ad nauseam*: one for an herbal prostate remedy, starring former NFL quarterback Joe Theisman, the other for investing in gold, starring the gray-haired, rugged-looking actor William Devane.

These campaigns are minting money with star power because people react irrationally to celebrities and celebrity endorsements. And at all levels, NetJets's sales improved as soon as Warren Buffett bought the company. Warren is a rich person's celebrity. He is not an expert in air travel safety. Levitra® was made popular beginning with ads starring former Chicago Bears coach Mike Ditka, a cigar-chomping tough guy—a man's man, but not an expert on medicine.

If people were rational, it would be better to promote NetJets with a highly credentialed expert in aircraft maintenance and to promote Levitra® with a top doctor from the Harvard Medical School.

I have used star power by association, rented star power, and manufactured star power throughout my business life, with celebrity endorsements from the likes of Joan Rivers and Fox Business economics expert Harry Dent. Top celebrity speakers such as Brian Tracy and Tom Hopkins have written introductions to books for me, and I even got an endorsement from a contestant on the TV show *The Apprentice* in which she says, "Even Donald Trump could learn a thing or two from Dan's book."

My authority status is what draws 1,000 to 1,500 entrepreneurs to our major GKIC events, and I welcome those that buy six, eight, or twenty books to be autographed and given to friends because they're working as a subtle sales force, reaching lots of people I might never reach otherwise, at no out-of-pocket cost, bringing new customers to GKIC and occasionally a client to me.

This authority status also draws others to me, who want to be associated with me through endorsements or even coauthorship of a book because this allows them to position themselves further in their own fields as experts and authorities.

I have also gotten a lot of speaking engagements on programs where I've appeared—often repeatedly—with an eclectic collection of political, business, and world leaders and Hollywood and sports celebrities. I've spent nine years with the famous SUCCESS events (held in sports arenas with audiences of ten thousand to thirty-five thousand), and I've attended many clients' events.

I often urge clients to hire celebrity speakers; at GKIC events, where we always use at least one celebrity entrepreneur, the list has included Gene

Simmons (KISS), Joan Rivers, Ivanka Trump, John Rich (winner, *Celebrity Apprentice*), and Barbara Corcoran (*Shark Tank*).

Because of my plan, I have been able to work with a lot of impressive people whose names should arguably not influence others' thinking about my value as an advisor on business or marketing matters. There is no rational link between my appearing on programs with these people and my expertise and trustworthiness as someone to tell you how to invest your money in advertising and marketing.

It should not be influential. But it is.

## Partial List of Celebrities, Authors, Business Leaders, & Others Dan Kennedy Has Appeared on Programs with as a Speaker

**Political & World Leaders**
President Gerald Ford*
President Ronald Reagan*
President George Bush*
President Donald Trump
Gen. Norman Schwarzkopf*
Secretary Colin Powell*
Mikail Gorbachev*
Lady Margaret Thatcher*
William Bennett*

**Legendary Entrepreneurs**
Mark McCormack*, (sports agent;
founder, IMG, author; *What They Don't
Teach You at Harvard Business School*)
Ben & Jerry*
(Ben & Jerry's Ice Cream)
Debbi Fields*
(Mrs. Fields Cookies)
Jim McCann*
(1-800-Flowers)
Joe Sugarman*
(Blu-Blockers)

**Hollywood Personalities &
Entertainers**
Johnny Cash
Naomi Judd*
Mary Tyler Moore*
Christopher Reeve*
The Smothers Brothers
Willard Scott*
Barbara Walters
Charlton Heston

**Broadcasters**
Larry King*
Paul Harvey*
Deborah Norville

**Authors & Speakers**
Zig Ziglar* *(See You at the Top)*
Brian Tracy*
Jim Rohn*
Tom Hopkins*
Mark Victor Hansen*
*(Chicken Soup for The Soul)*
Tony Robbins* *(Unlimited Power)*
Mike Vance* (dean, Disney Univ.;
author, *Think outside the Box*)
Michael Gerber *(E-Myth)*

**Sports Personalities, Athletes, &
Coaches**
Joe Montana*
Troy Aikman*
Peyton Manning*
Mike Singletarry
Coach Tom Landry*
Coach Jimmy Johnson*
Coach Lou Holtz*
Dick Vitale*
George Foreman*
Muhammad Ali*
Mary Lou Retton*
Bonnie Blair*
Dan Jansen

**Other Newsmakers**
Lt. Col. Oliver North
Gerry Spence*
Alan Dershowitz*
Capt. Scott O'Grady*

**Health**
Dr. Ted Broer*
Dr. Jack Groppel*

*Appeared with on multiple occasions*

## AUTHORITY MARKETING: THE TRIFECTA OF MAGNETIC ATTRACTION AND RISING INCOME

If you wish to achieve fame and status in your field, you must design and implement an Authority Marketing plan that includes multiple strategies—including book authorship—to position yourself as an undisputed expert, influential authority, and in-demand celebrity.

When you combine expert status, authority, and celebrity, you cash in a winning trifecta ticket. These three factors, working in concert, act to deliver three very desirable benefits: you are made able to more readily attract more and better clients/customers, make selling to them easier, and make price less of an issue so that the profitability of your business improves.

How do you achieve that trifecta most effectively and efficiently? With the power of Authority Marketing.

CHAPTER 1

# WHY SHOULD ANYONE LISTEN TO YOU?

I t's a fair question. What about you stands out from the crowd in your chosen profession? Why should anyone purchase your product or service, listen to your opinion over someone else in the same field, or search you out specifically for these things?

Because you are *the* authority.

Because prospective clients trust you more than your competition and because you know more than the other guys. Because you've established yourself as the leading authority in your field, and you have gone to great lengths to ensure that this is known to every one of your potential clients.

That is the power of Authority Marketing.

When Advantage|Forbes Books was started over ten years ago, we really thought we were in the book-selling business. And at first, we were. But what we realized over time is that we're not in the book business; we're really in the marketing business. And we're not just in the marketing business; we're in the Authority Marketing business.

Because establishing yourself as *the* authority, the thought leader, and the expert in your field—real estate, law, finance, or otherwise—is ultimately how you're able to command outsize influence over others and to dominate your competition.

Why should anyone listen to you? Because you are the authority on the subject, and in many cases, you "wrote the book" on the subject.

Becoming an authority in your specialty and in your community allows you to create an *unfair advantage* in the marketplace by immediately positioning you above others in the same field, and it *opens doors*, which leads to the exponential growth of your firm.

This book is not about writing and publishing a book. Yes, to solidify your place as an authority on any topic, authoring a book on the subject is often a mandatory step, but becoming the authority requires a more robust and strategic plan.

There are twenty-eight million businesses in America, but fewer than 4 percent ever surpass $1 million in annual revenue, while fewer than 0.4 percent ever surpass $10 million in annual revenue. Only seventeen thousand ever surpass $50 million in annual revenue. Why? Because they never get their marketing puzzle figured out.

Most financial professionals realize that clients choose their realtors, attorneys, and advisors based on relationships, not on the business itself. It's an emotional connection, and the greater the connection fostered between clients and their financial professional, the better chance that professional has of gaining a lifelong client.

Positioning yourself and your firm as *the* authority is the cornerstone of generating that emotional connection.

Are you ready to grow your firm? Are you ready to stand out in your field and become the authority in your industry? Are you ready to open more doors with potential clients than you ever imagined? Then read on and discover how Authority Marketing is the key to unlocking these opportunities and more.

CHAPTER 2

# BREAKING THROUGH THE BRICK WALL

I f you're this far in the book, you already understand the importance and value of building authority in your field.

Of the twenty-eight million businesses in the United States, those that surpass the $10 million and $50 million annual revenue milestones make it because they're focused singularly on one goal: hypergrowth. That is, the more doors they open, the more clients they will attract.

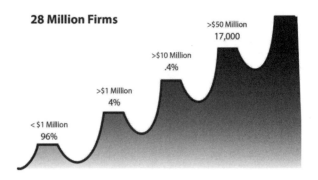

**28 Million Firms**

>$50 Million
17,000

>$10 Million
.4%

>$1 Million
4%

< $1 Million
96%

How do these companies achieve hypergrowth? How do they open those doors and keep opening them effectively?

By creating authority in their field and leveraging that authority to give them as many unfair advantages over their competition as possible.

## THE VALUE OF UNFAIR ADVANTAGES

By definition, an unfair advantage is *a unique way of organizing your thinking, communication, and action in more productive ways that competitors can neither comprehend nor copy.*

The greatest financial professionals are those who have created the largest number of unfair advantages for themselves. Take Warren Buffett, the "Oracle of Omaha," who enrolled at Columbia Business School in order to learn directly from investment guru Benjamin Graham. This was a wise decision—as was his early investment in a small firm called Berkshire Hathaway. Following the value investment philosophy of his teacher (with his own unique spin), he rapidly grew Berkshire Hathaway from a small textile manufacturer to one of the largest and most well-known conglomerates in the world. By the 1990s he was a billionaire, and he now stands as one of the richest men alive.

On perhaps a more relatable level, consider the practice of Jeanette Bajalia, who decided to create an affiliate company to her financial investment firm Petros Estate and Retirement Planning that focused on the distinct issues that women face in financial planning. To promote her new company, Jeanette then authored the book *Wi$e Up Women! A Guide to Total Fiscal and Physical Well-Being.*

"The book was written and published with the intent of being able to provide it to people as they indicated an interest… As a faith-based company we are very focused on educating first and using that as a primary means of generating interest."

The book established Jeanette as an authority and expert in the niche field of financial investing specifically for women and became a valuable resource as she began organizing workshops based on her unique financial planning approach. She also sends copies to clients, offers the book for free to callers on the national radio show "Coach Pete's Financial Safari," and leaves copies of it in the reception area of her offices for potential new clients to leaf through.

As her partner, Brian Mickley, explains, "As the person responsible for keeping a close eye on company finances, I was skeptical about spending money on a book because I was skeptical about the return. Then, I heard people talking about the book and I saw the many ways we were using it, and I said, 'You know, this wasn't such a bad deal after all.' Now, I would say we've already paid for the book a few times over with new clients and all the intangible benefits we've gotten from it."

By creating that unfair advantage of authority for herself and leveraging it with a deliberately implemented marketing plan, Jeanette dramatically differentiated himself from every other financial advisor in the area.

## AUTHORITY CAN BE MANUFACTURED

What every firm should understand is that authority does not happen blindly. It does not happen will-lessly. It does not creep up on you in the darkness of night. It happens over time, and it is deliberately created. Some methods for creating authority are through the establishment of past achievements, awards, professional designation, and experience.

Of course, you may spend half a lifetime building this line of authority for yourself when, out of the blue, another person in your profession with less than half of your experience may skyrocket past you in authority ranking.

This "super authority" may seem sudden to others, but it's the product of deliberate actions, of positioning yourself in a broad range of effective marketing campaigns (see more on these in Chapter 6: The Seven Pillars of Authority Marketing), and of using unfair advantages to outflank and distance yourself from the competition.

Simply put, authority can be—and often is—manufactured.

## AUTHORITY TO BUILD TRUST

Advantage | ForbesBooks Authors Matt Zagula and Dan Kennedy authored a book a few years back titled *How to Create Trust in an Understandably Untrustworthy World*. Trust, while the most important part of gaining a client, is also the most difficult to achieve, and by positioning yourself and your firm as trustworthy—and specifically more trustworthy than your competition—you win business and feed into the acceleration of your firm's hypergrowth.

Trust, according to Matt and Dan, can be built on a number of factors, each of which is a valuable component of an effective Authority Marketing plan because trust, to clients, is essentially interchangeable with authority.

Take Dan's examples of Joe Theisman and William Devane in the foreword on "The Irrational Reaction to Star Power." In Dan's own words, these icons "are minting money with star power because people react irrationally to celebrities and celebrity endorsements."

People see the status of being well-known as a basis for trust. Therefore, if you're well-known as an expert in your field, then you've established that first essential connection with your clients.

In order to build trust, however, you must be "out there" on multiple levels, not just with a book, but through campaigns embracing every type of media, including word-of-mouth, to the point where if someone in your target market hasn't heard of you, they've almost certainly been living without contact from the outside world for far too long.

We go into several of the most valuable components of an effective Authority Marketing strategy in Chapter 6: The Seven Pillars of Authority Marketing, but briefly, establishing that trust/authority in your field requires a solid marketing campaign focusing on all aspects of media consumption, from blogging to radio shows to press releases to event hosting.

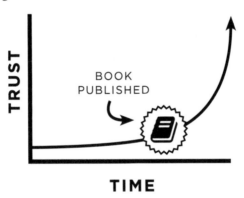

It may seem like a large hurdle at first, but keep in mind that an effective marketing campaign is not implemented in one full-on attack but rather over time, building on each smaller success to achieve greater ones until it almost becomes a self-perpet-uating cycle.

By building on this essential value of trust and ac-celerating your trust value through the development and growth of you and your firm's authority, you can double, triple, and even quadruple the response rate of all the marketing you are doing. Authority and trust amplify the results of your marketing.

And the more trust you gain, the more likely it is that potential clients will purposefully seek you out and so on, propelling your clients into that all-too-coveted position of hypergrowth.

# CHAPTER 3

# CLIENTS SHOULD COME TO YOU, NOT THE OTHER WAY AROUND

**I**f you've ever been offshore fishing for blue marlin, you know that this six hundred-plus-pound behemoth is one of the most difficult saltwater fish to catch in the world. Landing one requires tremendous skill and just the right bait.

Now, if we were to offer you two options for catching blue marlin—a fishing net or a precisely tuned outrigger-led fishing line with just the right blue marlin bait or lure—which would you take?

It seems like an obvious answer, but when you relate it to hypergrowing your firm, it's amazing how many people choose to go with the net when it comes to marketing and building their authority. Instead of putting something out there that their exact target market is desperate to have (or giving the impression that they *absolutely have to have it*), they instead take a big old net and sling it as best they can into the water, hoping to draw up something good.

To further the analogy, throwing a big, heavy, soaking wet net into the ocean time and again can wear you out quickly, whereas sitting patiently with a line is a more strategic (and enjoyable) process. Then, when the prospective fish is snagged, you put everything you have into it because you know that the exact fish you want is on the other end of that line.

So why are you wearing out your arms throwing a net over and over again into murky water? Why aren't you developing just the right bait and strategically positioning yourself so that your target clients come to you?

## THE MAGNET PRINCIPLE

If you're attracting your target client, turning yourself into a magnet instead of casting around for whatever's about, then you will ultimately attract better people and better opportunities to you and your firm. As an authority, you are the shiny bait in the water that fish swim toward. No net required.

This principle goes beyond the client, as well. To hypergrow your firm, you need to attract far more than just your target clients. You also need to attract all-star employees to help you build that relationship and develop the invaluable trust needed to grow and retain your client base, and you need to attract publicity, media, and speaking opportunities to continue building your authority.

Are desirable employees and opportunities attracted to you? Do clients come to you instead of the other way around? Can you command the way you run your firm without your clients blinking an eye because they trust you implicitly? If not, then you need to drop the net and start learning how to fish.

# CHAPTER 4

# WHAT IS AUTHORITY MARKETING?

**B**y definition, Authority Marketing is the **strategic process** of **systematically positioning** a person or an organization as the leader and expert in their industry, community, and marketplace to **command outsize influence over all competitors.**

There are a few key terms here, which we've highlighted in the definition. The first is "strategic process."

Strategic process means creating a deliberate plan that is executed over a period of time. There is no "What do we need to do today?" or "How should we tackle this next month?" Authority Marketing requires a carefully defined blueprint that is implemented methodically over time because, as we've said before, no authority is gained immediately by random chance and without deliberate intention.

Next is "systematic positioning." Part-and-parcel of strategic process, "systematic positioning" means implementing your plan in such a way that it provides the most effective return on investment possible. If you're a CPA firm in Cleveland, Ohio, you're not going to try to get on the main cable news networks in Minneapolis or Pittsburgh. You're not going to pitch news stories to the *Detroit Free Press*. Rather, you focus your efforts in your firm's prime radius, and you work to ensure that you are known in *every* aspect of that area's media channels. You don't just want people to recognize your firm's name, you want them to see or hear your name and say, "Hey, I've been hearing a lot about those guys."

Finally, the last key term is to "command outsize influence over all competitors." This is where your unfair advantages come into play. You must position your authority so that when people think of your industry, the first name that comes to mind is you and your firm. If prospects trust you more than the other guys, you win the business. If potential clients think you know more than the other guys or your firm is the expert over the other guys, you win them as clients.

At the end of the day, when you're competing in a marketplace, an industry, and a community, it's all about the sway that you have over and above other firms to influence prospects toward your services.

Entrepreneur Ben Compaine once said, "The marketplace is not a podium in a quiet lecture hall, where everyone gets a turn to speak. It's more like a crowded bazaar in Casablanca. You must distract people from their main occupation—living—and show them that they can't live a minute longer without one of your beautiful rugs."

When you and your firm are *the* authority, you have a powerful microphone and platform in that crowded bazaar, which makes all the difference.

Authority Marketing, then, is a very systematic, very deliberate plan to position yourself and your firm as the expert that people want to serve their housing, legal, and investment needs, and it's all about becoming a magnet that's attracting potential clients to you, versus you having to forcefully attract them.

## THE JIM ZEIGLER RULE

Authority Marketing is also about fame. For any of you who are deterred by the idea of seeking fame, let us offer you one piece of advice: this isn't about ego.

Fame, when it comes to Authority Marketing, is not about you: it's about your name as a brand, your name as an authority, and your potential clients' perception that you and your firm are who they want to give money to. It's about being famous where you need to be famous because people have an irrational reaction to celebrity. When you're well-known, people and potential clients not only tend to trust you, but they also flock to you. We go into this a little more in Chapter 5, and Dan touched on this irrational reaction to stardom in the foreword to this book, but in sum, if people were rational, they wouldn't rely on John Madden's advice when considering athlete's foot treatments, or they would carefully pick their face-care product instead of going with

Adam Levine and Sarah Michelle Gellar's recommendation to use Proactiv.

It's about fame, which is something that the figureheads of any firm need to accept if they're going to hypergrow their business, but it's not about being famous on a movie star kind of level. It's about being famous where it matters: in your marketplace, in your industry, and in your community.

Let us tell you a quick story. We have an author at Advantage by the name of Jim Zeigler. He is a consultant to automobile dealers, and he said something to us years ago that has stuck with us ever since.

"Harper and Adam," he said, "outside of the car business, nobody knows who I am. But inside the car business, I'm a friggin' rock star."

Being known and respected by people that aren't in your industry, marketplace, or community doesn't matter. They aren't the ones who are going to give you money. It doesn't matter to Jim if someone in the construction industry or the healthcare industry knows him from a stick in the road, because those people would never need his services.

When building your own authority, you don't need to be a worldwide celebrity. You *do* need to be *the* authority in your industry, in your community, and in the marketplace where you and your firm live because you need people who have the ability and willingness to give you money and to see you as *the* authority.

You need to be famous, slightly.

## ROCK STARS OF AUTHORITY MARKETING

Let us give you three very different examples of professionals who have very successfully used Authority Marketing to their advantage. We'll start with arguably the most famous of the three . . . unless you live in Denver, Colorado, that is.

## SUZE ORMAN

If you're in the financial services industry, forget for just a
minute any opinion you may
have about Suze Orman, because the fact of the matter is that,
as a financial advisor, she's "made it."

Ten years ago, Suze was just another small fish in a
sea of one hundred and sixty thousand other financial advisors trying to make their way in a fiercely
competitive industry.

She was doing speaking engagements and participating in programs in her community, but she was
doing little else to make herself stand out from the
crowd.

Then she self-published a book, and she promoted
that book hard. That book led to some media appearances that gradually grew to appearances on national television and radio shows, and because she
was able to portray herself as calm and personable,

people saw her and felt like she was speaking the truth; they felt like they could trust her.

Suze was able to take all those little pieces of success and build them into more success so that, now, Suze isn't a financial advisor anymore. She's a media personality who's authored at least ten books and several multimedia kits on everything from wills and trusts to identity theft. She has a weekly television show on CNBC, and she speaks all over the country.

## MATT ZAGULA

Matt Zagula is not your ordinary financial advisor.

Licensed in all fifty states, Matt maintains a busy personal practice, but he doesn't just stop at financial advising. He's taken it a few steps further by becoming a master coach to elite financial advisors and attorneys across the country.

Then, to promote his business, attract clients, and help close sales, he decided to author not just one book but several, penning some on his own and others with co-authors, including *Invasion of the Money Snatchers, Don't Fumble Your Retirement with Rocky Bleier,* and *Creating Trust* with Dan Kennedy.

At every chance, Matt uses his books to market his business. He sends books in the mail, offers listeners books during radio interviews, and promotes books on social media. He also hosts "evenings with the author" instead of the traditional financial seminars. In anything he does, his books make a lasting impression with potential clients because, as he says, "people don't throw books away." While his books attract new clients to his firm, referrals from these clients provide "astronomical" returns. Matt simply gives each new client two books along with a *Consumer's Guide to Finding the Right Advice Giver.* He will then say, "If you have friends, family, or neighbors with financial issues, just hand them a book and our guide and tell them, 'These are the people we like and trust.'"

Authoring *Creating Trust* with nationally renowned marketing guru Dan Kennedy was one of Matt's first orders of business when he decided to expand into the coaching business. While it provided helpful advice on establishing trust with clients, it was also a tool to attract top financial advisors to a two-day event that featured both Matt and Dan and focused on the key points of creating trust in the financial industry.

As a result of the campaign they created, both Matt and Dan saw a seven-figure annualized business over the next few years. Equally interesting are the results for the coaching group participants. From their group of sixty, forty-five went on to write and market books for their businesses. As Matt notes, "that resulted in forty-five business owners increasing their collective businesses by $132 million year over year … for most of them that probably represents at least a 20 to 30 percent increase."

When you write your book with a purpose in mind, Matt says, "You can drive revenue, drive productivity, and be successful by communicating your message." Whatever your purpose may be, you can generate leads at a level that suits you and your business.

## ANN VANDERSLICE

In an often-crowded profession, standing out often means finding a unique niche to hang your hat on. This is exactly what Ann Vanderslice did when she decided to take her retirement planning financial services one step further by specializing in retirement planning specifically for federal employees. And, with several federal offices in her town of Denver, Colorado, Ann had a small but ready market to cater to. As her practice began to grow to the limits of that pool, however, Ann knew she needed to expand her reach and take her unique financial services angle from hyper-local to the national stage.

"I'm pretty well recognized in the Colorado area as an expert in federal benefits," said Anne, "but I wanted that expanded to a national view."

So, in January 2012, Ann published her first book, *FedTelligence: The Ultimate Guide to Mastering Your Federal Benefits.*

By uniquely branding herself, Ann was able to gain authority in a focused market on a much broader scale, and she now does up to eighty speaking engagements a year both in her hometown and around the country, thanks in large part to her book.

"Federal benefits are a complicated topic," says Ann. "Because of that complexity, you need to be able to break it down into simple terms, and that's really what I do—I break it down. My book is written just like I speak so when people say, 'I've been to your class and wanted to go back and review,' it's easy for them to do that. They'll tell me, 'this sounds just like you,' because I describe everything just like I would in the office or in the seminar."

Promoting her unique niche in this way has also helped her develop a small but highly focused fan base, which has played a significant role in driving referrals to her.

"I know my clients will get the book and then they'll tell their coworkers, 'Oh, you've got to read this.' I've even had one woman at the US Mint buy about a dozen copies. She pays me for them, and then she sells them to friends at work."

Of course, effective Authority Marketing doesn't require that you become wildly famous, just slightly famous, as Ann became in the field of retirement planning for federal employees. However, if you choose to continue to strategically plan and systematically position yourself beyond your slight celebrity status, you could gain authority beyond your defined audience to a statewide or even nationwide authority.

But ask someone like Ann how being slightly famous is treating her, and she'll probably tell you that she already has far more business than she can handle—which is a problem we're all aiming to have.

# CHAPTER 5

# FOUR REASONS FOR AUTHORITY MARKETING

**D**an Kennedy, the author of this book's foreword and known direct marketing expert, has been using Authority Marketing for the better part of his forty-year professional career, and over that time he's developed what he likes to call "The Four Reasons for Authority Marketing." These are:

1. Be known where you live.

2. Be the one everyone wants to go to for a high-value product or service.

3. Be the person whom others of influence want to stand next to.

4. Leverage your authority for autonomy.

These four reasons are the goals that any financial professional looking to hypergrow his or her firm should have.

Paul McCartney once commented that he and John Lennon used to say to each other, "Now, let's write a swimming pool."

They said this because they had earned such a level of authority as singer-songwriters that they could sit down, put pen to paper, and shortly thereafter have sold whatever ditty they worked up for at least the cost of a new swimming pool.

That ability to have *income at will* is the power of Authority Marketing.

Is your firm to the point where you can generate income at will? If not, then it's time to learn how to develop these four essential factors so that you can push your practice up, over, and rocketing past your current revenue plateau and into some serious hypergrowth.

## REASON #1: BE KNOWN WHERE YOU LIVE

Being known where you live doesn't always mean geographically. It means achieving familiarity and recognition where your clients live—whether that's within a tri-state area or in a specific real estate, legal, or financial field.

In essence, this first reason for Authority Marketing is what Jim Zeigler meant when he said that, "Outside of the car business, nobody knows who I am. But inside of the car business, I'm a friggin' rock star."

For Jim, all that mattered was that others in the car industry knew who he was and purposefully pursued him for his services.

For our financial friend Ann Vanderslice, the vast majority of her clientele are from Colorado, so why care about being known beyond that point?

If you're a financial advisor in Denver, you don't need to be famous in California. You don't even need to be famous in the rest of the state. If your clients are located nationally or internationally, you don't need to be known to everyone, only to your target audience who has the capacity to do business with you. Pursuing fame for any wider an audience is a fool's errand and is only done for the sake of ego.

## REASON #2: BE THE ONE EVERYONE WANTS TO GO TO

In a field of sameness, you need to be the financial professional that people prefer to go to. The key to this second reason relates back to the first reason for Authority Marketing—you want to be the one whom everyone wants to go to for your services, but you don't necessarily need to be known by those who wouldn't use your services. You need to be known as the authority in your specific community, industry, and marketplace, whether that's on an international basis in a specific field, such as the best financial advisor for professional football players, or on a hometown level if your business is geographically defined, like Ann Vanderslice's. You need to be known only on the levels and in the fields where your clients exist.

And that's really the big idea. This is why it's so important to be slightly famous. You could spend gobs of money trying to be well-known in your firm across broad areas, but doing so is the same as casting that net over and over again into an opaque sea. Without a target, that tremendous effort is almost entirely wasted, and you are spending money with no ability to recoup that investment. But if you choose the right lure and focus on the places where you know your potential clients live, then your efforts are going to pay off.

Take Advantage Author Thomas Helbig. A year before he wrote his book *The Boomer's Guide to a Worry-Free Retirement*, Thomas had a financial planning business that was keeping him busy but it wasn't quite as successful as he wanted it to be. One year after publishing his book, Thomas's income doubled, and he's been featured in spots on America's Premier Experts, *Forbes, The Wall Street Journal*, and USA Today, as well as on two radio programs: Dana Loesch's "The Dana Show," and Coach Pete's "Financial Safari."

As he says, "I have doubled my income because of the book and I hope to triple it." And he has experienced additional benefits as an author that he appreciates almost as much. For one, Thomas finds that new clients "look at him in a different light." He finds they are more relaxed, and they seem to trust him more. In addition to this, Thomas notes another benefit: "It has given me more confidence in my business to say I'm a best-selling author. I feel more confident than I ever have. So, the book has changed my life."

And that, ultimately, is one of the top goals of any business: to be the place that people go out of their way to work with.

## REASON #3: BE THE PERSON WHOM OTHERS OF INFLUENCE WANT TO STAND NEXT TO

This leads us to the third reason for Authority Marketing. By making yourself and your firm known in your marketplace, in your community, and in your industry, people will want to associate with you. They will want to brag about being associated with you or about being a client of yours, and consequently, people of greater and greater influence will want to be seen with you.

This becomes a self-perpetuating cycle. The more people of note who are seen with you, the more well-known you become, and the more people of increasingly greater influence want to be seen with you, then the more visibility you have with the general public. This leads to the subconscious association that, "Well, if such-and-such likes them, then they must be good."

When you attract the right people to yourself and your firm, you bring more deals in, and that's the goal.

## REASON #4: LEVERAGE YOUR AUTHORITY FOR AUTONOMY

With these three factors in play—people knowing who you are, people going out of their way to become your clients, and people of influence standing next to you and increasing your visibility, notoriety, and appeal—you are able to achieve the ultimate fourth reason for Authority Marketing: leveraging your authority for autonomy.

The more of an authority figure you are in your industry, marketplace, and community, the more negotiating power you have and the higher the fees you can command without people balking or comparing you to others. And that, at the end of the day, is what it's really all about. It's the reason we're entrepreneurs and private firm owners.

How do you build an Authority Marketing plan? The process is different for everyone, but everyone who is successful at it aims to hit a minimum of seven main focus areas, which we'll call the Seven Pillars of Authority Marketing.

# CHAPTER 6

# THE SEVEN PILLARS OF AUTHORITY MARKETING

**T**here are many ways to build an effective Authority Marketing plan beyond these focus areas, but if you're going to put the time and effort into developing your authority and developing it properly, you'll need to have a solid presence in each of the following Seven Pillars:

## PILLARS OF AUTHORITY MARKETING

 BRANDING & OMNIPRESENCE

 REFERRAL MARKETING

 CONTENT MARKETING

 LEAD GENERATION

 PR & MEDIA

SPEAKING

EVENTS

# 1. BRANDING & OMNIPRESENCE

Most people know what brand is. You have a logo, you have a color scheme, and you may even have a motto. But that's for your firm. What about you? What's your personal brand? If we typed your-name-dot-com into my site search bar, what would come up? Would it be a website listing your achievements, recent awards, charitable outreach, and the books you've written, or would it lead us to a completely unrelated site about squirrel feeders or, maybe worse, nothing at all?

Building brand isn't just about building your practice's brand but also your personal brand. And you not only need to do those part-and-parcel with each other, but you also need to do so universally. In order for your audience to recall your name, it must be clearly recognizable and associated in their mind. For an individual, this includes character traits such as integrity and charisma, as well as your skills and earned credentials.

Before you can create visual images, logos, and on-line copy to showcase who you are, you must distill your personal brand into what makes you unique. This will be different for everyone, but a few key factors will help you discover your brand. Consider how your *personal mission* may separate you from the masses, like, "Help ten thousand people get clean water," or "Eliminate bad hires." Your *philosophy* or approach to life may differentiate you, like financial advisor Brady Raanes, who founded (c)3 Wines in Napa Valley as a way of creating opportunity for those in need. One hundred percent of his winery's profits go to nonprofits around the world, focusing particularly on organizations that concentrate on sustainable solutions to global issues.

Your *journey* may be the most memorable aspect of your brand, especially if you overcame a great obstacle to become successful. Many experts focus on their teachings or *science*—the insight and knowledge that only you have in your industry. Finally, your *tribe* or community may be a highlight of your personal brand. If you led the championship football team or served on the National Association of Personal Financial Advisors board, then you have personal brand qualities as a leader of a group.

Well-known leaders are very clear about who they are and what image they convey to their audience. They work hard to reinforce their best qualities in every communication about them, whether it is a radio interview, an article quote, or their online profiles.

## 2. CONTENT MARKETING

Content marketing is how you build that omnipresence. You and/or your team need to be committed to creating a significant amount of high-quality content written specifically for your prospective clients. This content can come in multiple forms. Most significantly, of course, is authorship of a book, but there are also white papers, special reports, articles, blog posts, webinars, teleseminars, and podcasts, to name a few. The focus should be on creating rich content for social media and constantly sharing valuable information with your target clients. As you create appreciable content, you also create a legion of fans that are excited to consume what you create.

The content you create serves a specific purpose: to educate your prospects and clients. Your content should build trust and credibility, so it is very important that your statements are accurate and helpful. Each piece you create should help your prospective client answer a question or learn more about your services. Savvy content marketers create sequences of content, strategically linked from one topic to the next, to stimulate the reader to engage more. The more engaged your audience is, the more likely you are to convert them to becoming a loyal client.

Of course, you may know your stuff and can write tons of content about what you do, but is it content your audience wants to read? One mistake many financial professionals make is writing advanced articles about their topic when their client is still in the initial stages of research and needs a 101 lesson. To be an authority, you must know your topic inside and out and be able to translate it into the right language that will resonate with your audience.

Finally, there is timing. You must be consistent with your content or it loses its effectiveness. You don't want them to forget you! Content marketing is about being top of mind when your prospective client is ready to choose a realtor, lawyer, or an advisor, so you need regular, well-timed content. If there is a new trend or recent news story that affects your firm, get your perspective out to your audience before someone else does. Be their go-to source for great information, and they will return to you for advice as the true thought leader in the field.

## 3. PR & MEDIA

Getting your name and your firm's name mentioned in media is important because most people don't believe what you say about yourself, but they'll believe what others have to say about you.

More importantly, they believe what major media has to say about you. The authority that comes when you're featured or interviewed on radio, TV, magazines, or newspapers is significant because it helps with omnipresence. Additionally, having all of these mentions across multiple media platforms also helps to build your online presence, or what's known as your "digital footprint."

If we Googled your name, for instance, would we have to pack a lunch?

Think about that for a second. What we mean is, would it take us so much time to go through all of the results that come up that we could eat lunch while doing it? If the answer is no, then you have an Authority Marketing problem that needs to be solved.

In the age of commerce that we live in, Google is a vehicle for decision making. If your presence online doesn't dominate the competition, then you lose. This is why content marketing and branding are so valuable. They see your firm mentioned in media, they visibly associate with the logo, and when they search for you online, they find a bevy of information, including other media outlets mentioning you.

The fact of the matter is that the mass public trusts the mainstream media. Whether you appear on CNBC or on a local radio station, people will assume that you're an authority—because why else would these outlets invite you on as a guest? It's irrational, but again, there's nothing rational about the general public's decision-making process.

Marketing is about perception and, hopefully, that perception is built on reality. But people buy the perception, not the reality, and as you build your authority, the perception is that you are the number-one go-to person in your field.

## 4. SPEAKING

Are you currently speaking to groups that consist of your target audience? If not, and if you're uncomfortable with speaking with at least some regularity, you need to find someone else in your firm with whom you're comfortable putting into a position of authority. Because speaking, bar none, is the best way to enforce your authority position and generate high-quality leads.

As a speaker, people automatically assume you're an expert or they—the university, company, or organization putting on the seminar—wouldn't have invited you to speak. Secondly, if what you say is competent, polished, and professional, you will connect with a subset of the audience as though you were lovers at first sight. They'll want to speak with you afterward and do business with you. We can tell you from personal experience that there will be at least two or three people waiting in line to talk with you after every speech made, and all of them want to know how they can do business with you.

## 5. LEAD GENERATION

Some of you may be asking, "What does Authority Marketing have to do with lead generation?" Everything, in fact, because it's far easier to generate leads when you're seen as an authority. Back to one of the points Dan made in the foreword to this book: are you still selling, or can you prescribe to people what they need? As an authority, you can tell people what they need, and they'll do it. But if you come at them looking and acting like a salesperson, they'll ditch you faster than a toupee in a windstorm.

The easiest way to generate high-quality leads is to have something that the lead wants, including information that they find valuable. Whether you do this in the form of a book or through consistent blogging, podcasts, webinars, or any of the other various forms of direct-to-client marketing, the goal is to get in front of as many prospective clients as possible. This leads to omnipresence, which leads to authority.

## 6. REFERRAL MARKETING

How do you stimulate and encourage your satisfied clients to refer you to others? It's a tricky and delicate question that most firms screw up.

What would you say if we asked you, "If your most loyal clients went to a cocktail party, would they brag about you to their friends?"

That's another one of the main goals of Authority Marketing: to build a persona with you and your firm so that clients brag to friends about you.

Referral marketing falls into two types: client referrals and referrals from influencers.

Client referrals are the most common and are an outcome of great services. Hosting a client appreciation party is a best practice used by authority marketers who want to thank their best clients and ask them for an introduction to their friends and family.

An often-missed opportunity is the referrals from influencers—more specifically, a target list of people who are in front of a group of your prospective clients every day. For an estate attorney, for example, this may be business associations or financial advisors. Once you've identified the influencers who have the ability to refer clients to you, you must make it overly simple for them to refer. Have you ever gotten a letter in the mail from a charity with a self-addressed stamped envelope inside for you to mail back your donation? It's the same principle.

Most people want to refer a client to you, but they get busy in the everyday. Make it easy for your influencers by giving them the tools they need to refer you. Tools may include a script for how to talk about you and your services, a brochure or whitepaper about what you do, a published book, or a specific landing page to learn more. Most important is to educate your influencers on when to refer you, citing key issues or concerns they might hear that your firm addresses.

For both client and influencer referrals, it must be a systematic, turnkey process. Authority marketers know how many referrals they receive each year and set goals to grow this number every year by investing in those relationships and thanking the referrer.

Referral marketing is relationship marketing at its best.

## 7. EVENTS

Before we talk about events, let us start by saying that real estate, law, and financial firms are most successful when they have loyal tribes of clients, which can be created, in great part, through effective content marketing.

The most successful fims have tribes of clients, and they create these tribes because they build relationships by *engaging their clients to the highest level possible.* This is important because engagement signifies loyalty, and loyalty signifies continued support and return to your firm.

Events, then, are where these loyal tribes can come together. The Carolinas Credit Union League in Columbia, South Carolina, for example, hosts "Financial Literacy Day," which brings together volunteers, high school students, and lawmakers to talk about the impact money has on our lives and how to manage money effectively.

Holding regular or annual events is one of the best ways to upsell, build additional loyalty, and expose more people to your tribe, making it a contagious and positive force for good.

Those, in a nutshell, are the Seven Pillars, and you can see how each relates back to the other. Every aspect feeds into the next, and all of it comes together to create a mass of positive marketing that, when implemented well and deliberately over time, leads to the ongoing and growing generation of authority and, ultimately, an influx of clients that allows you to run your firm on your own terms and only with those clients that you want to work with.

# CHAPTER 7

# AUTHORITY BY DESIGN: A CASE STUDY

**H**ow do you implement Authority Marketing for both yourself and your firm? In Chapter 4, we defined Authority Marketing as the **strategic process** of **systematically positioning** a person or an organization as the leader and expert in their industry, community, and marketplace **to command outsize influence over all competitors**.

Advantage author Charlie Epstein is an excellent example of Authority Marketing in action. While every business owner has his or her own way of approaching Authority Marketing, Charlie created an Authority Marketing strategy that has propelled him to authority status in the 401(k) industry. In the following chapter, Charlie outlines how authority marketing has helped him achieve star power in the financial field. We consider his story a case study in Authority Marketing at its best.

With more than thirty-five years of experience in the financial services industry, Charlie Epstein has been named by 401kWire as one of the top one hundred most influential people in the retirement industry, as well as one of the top three hundred most influential retirement plan advisors in the United States. He is the principal of Epstein Financial Group, LLC, and Epstein Financial Services, a registered investment advisory firm, although he's likely more well known for his two books, *Paychecks for Life* and *Save America, Save*, as well as his retirement plan professionals' coaching program, 401(k) Coach. Nationally, more than four thousand financial professionals have participated in Charlie's 401(k) coaching program, which offers training to develop the skills, systems, and processes necessary to excel in the 401(k) industry.

This is Charlie's story, in his own words.

## CREATING THE ULTIMATE
## UNFAIR ADVANTAGE

Being a published author is the ultimate unfair advantage for financial advisors, especially considering the competition we're all up against today. It's an advantage that has paid for itself many times over, and it's something I wish I'd thought to do much earlier in my career. As it was, I had to struggle through those first ten years or so just like everyone else, until I landed on my first idea for standing out in an increasingly crowded industry.

The 401(k) Coach program began in 2002 out of necessity. My partner at the time and I were in the process of building a third-party administrative firm from scratch with one of the largest accounting firms in our backyard of Holyoke, Massachusetts, when it occurred to us that we were up against some pretty steep competition. There were already two well-embedded TPA firms in the area, which meant that the only way we were going to stand out was to do something drastically different from those guys. Somewhere along the line it struck me that if we could just teach financial professionals who can't even spell 401(k) to sell 401(k), maybe they would be beholden to us and use our administrative services. That was the genesis of 401(k) Coach.

The first thing we did was to put out an email to local financial professionals—mostly in the insurance industry since Mass Mutual was practically in our backyard. Since I'd started with Mass Mutual back in 1979 as an insurance professional, we got about forty people to come to an introductory session to the 401(k) Coach program, during which we asked them to take a leap of faith with us. For $2,000, we explained, we would meet with them every ninety days for a year and help them grow their business.

I already had the first ninety days built an eight-hour course ready to go—knowing that I'd have to spend the next ninety days coming up with the next course and then the next one. As it turned out, we did so much business through those forty advisors that we became the number-one TPA in the country for Mass Mutual for small- to medium-size product. We put close to seventy plans on the books in that first year and realized that maybe we were on to something. Thus, 401(k) Coach was officially born.

Ten years later, in 2012, I wrote my first book, *Paychecks for Life* and shortly thereafter discovered the unfair advantage of being an author— an advantage that has made me several million dollars and counting in a relatively short period of time.

"Being an author has definitely been a game changer in my business! I've closed four 401(k) plans, totaling in excess of $80M, without even having my book in-hand. In each of these cases, I closed by saying, "Everything that I've just reviewed with you is in my new book, which is coming out next month. As soon as it does I will send you a copy." One new client ($29M plan) even asked if I would autograph it for him. The 401(k) Coach Accelerator Author System will make you an author faster, easier, and bigger than you can do on your own and it will set you apart from your competition. I most recently closed a $48M plan using my author status, beating out five other competitors. If you want to become the authority, the expert, even the celebrity in your marketplace, and create instant super credibility for yourself, I encourage you to check out The 401(k) Coach Accelerator Author System!"

—Joseph Ablahani, Capital Benefits, LLC

## ESTABLISHING *SUPER* CREDIBILITY

Think about when you first started in the business as an advisor. You had no credibility. Nobody knew who you were and no one cared.

*You* didn't even really know what you were doing.

But then, over the next ten to fifteen years— or in cases like mine, over the next thirty-five years—you worked diligently to increase your credibility in the marketplace. For financial advisors focusing on qualified retirement plans and life insurance, that meant that you probably went out and got your AIF and QKA designations—or your CLU, CHFC, CFP designations in the financial services and insurance industry; you went to conferences and got listed in the top hundred or top ten for financial advisors; and you accumulated accolades and plaques of recognition, all for the purpose of building credibility in the marketplace.

Of course, these are all great things to have, but the prerequisite to having them is *time*.

It takes a lot of time to build up this kind of credibility, and if you're just starting out in this business, you may not have that time to spend. Then you also have to factor in the credibility of your competition, who probably has the same designations as you, the same tools, and the same client pool, which pretty much puts you back to zero.

So how do you stand out? How do you crack that credibility line early or, if you're established but battling against other firms of equal credibility, how do you stand out? How do you create *super* credibility?

You become an author.

Writing a book is the fastest way to move from simply being yet another accredited advisor to that vaulted status of super credibility. And it happens instantaneously.

Let me give you an example. In early 2017 I was at a conference in California. The first night of the event, my wife and I found ourselves chatting with an interesting couple in the hotel lounge. In the course of the conversation I asked what he did and it turned out that he owned a manufacturing company just an hour down the road from my office.

Then he asked what I did.

"Well," I said, "I'm known nationally as the 401(k) Coach."

"What's that?" he asked.

I gave him the elevator pitch of the program and then said, "and I've also written two books, *Paychecks for Life* and *Save America, Save.*"

He seemed surprised. "You've written two books?"

"Yeah," I said. "Let me get you a copy. I might have one up in my room."

Of course, I'd brought about two cases of my books with me for the conference, so later that evening I grabbed a copy of *Save America, Save* from my room, wrote a short note in the cover, and had the concierge hand-deliver it to the man's hotel room.

Flash forward the next two and a half days of the conference and I don't see the guy again until the very last day. Then, as we're crossing the lounge to leave, he and his wife appear and make a bee-line for me.

"I've been looking for you!" he said. "I read your book."

"I think we're going to be seeing a lot more of you," his wife added.

By the time I got back to Massachusetts, the CFO of his company had already sent over all of their financial information. Then a quick follow-up conversation with the owner led to him revealing that, before he'd read my book, he'd been considering going with a 401(k) program created by none other than Tony Robbins.

Now, Tony Robbins is a giant. He's incredibly credible. But because I'd written a book, that potential client saw me as credible, too—credible enough to win his business. That's the power of becoming an author—the power of super credibility.

## YOUR ACE IN THE HOLE

Another benefit of becoming an author is that it automatically bestows on you the credibility trifecta: authority, celebrity, and expertise, otherwise known as the ACE Formula.

When I became an author for the first time with *Paychecks For Life*, my goal was to help clients figure out how to create paychecks for life, but the fallout—the big surprise of writing a book—was how much writing a book changed me in the eyes of the consumer. I was suddenly elevated to a position of authority and expertise. I stopped selling.

All I had to do was hand out the book and people would call.

As for the celebrity aspect, l learned quickly that the well-known adage is true, "The higher up in income you go, the more you are paid for who you are rather than for what you do."

Shortly after *Paychecks for Life* came out I was preparing a services plan for a reputable medical practitioner who'd read the book and contacted me because of it. We'd scheduled a dinner together to go over it and just beforehand I remember looking at myself in the mirror and saying, "Charlie, you're the expert. You're the authority, and she believes in you … and you believe in you, too."

So when the conversation that night finally got around to cost, I tripled the normal annual fee and she didn't even blink. I was hired.

## BETTER THAN A BUSINESS CARD

When you're looking to stand out with a potential client, a business card and brochure simply aren't going to cut it. There are tons of brochures out there, and more than likely, whoever gets one is going to toss it out without looking at it.

But who tosses out a book?

Take, for instance, a sales call that I went on with one of our new young advisors. Before we even called the company, we'd mailed the owner a copy of my book so that when we did call, the owner not only accepted the call, he also set up an appointment with us.

What really surprised me was that when we walked in, the business owner had my book sitting front and center on his desk. When was the last time you walked into a meeting and saw your brochure sitting on the potential client's desk? He'd not only hung onto it, but he actually apologized for not being able to read all of it before our meeting.

The benefit of the book didn't stop there, either. Later on in the meeting he asked a question that concerned one of the chapters in the book, so instead of explaining it in full I reached over, picked up the book, flipped to the chapter in question, and said, "See? This is exactly what I'm talking about. Read this chapter and we'll follow up."

Just the simple fact that so many of his answers were already explained in the book I'd given him went miles in establishing my authority and conveyed far more information than I could have through one, or even several, conversations.

Another case in point concerned a $15 million retirement plan that I was trying to land business with. Now, in the 401(k) world, you're typically trying to get in the door of a company by talking to the head of HR or the CFO. You're not talking directly with the decision makers or trustees at that point. In this case, I'd sent a copy of my book to the head of HR who read it and said to me, "These trustees need what you have."

Now, this HR director had only been with the company for six months, but he was onboard with us and he wanted to get the trustees onboard with us, as well. But because he was so new, he explained that bringing them onboard would likely take some time.

Fortunately, I had four more copies of the book with me at that meeting, so I offered them to him, saying, "Would it be helpful if you just gave my book to the other trustees?"

Eight months later we followed up with that company and they said they were booking a meeting between the trustees and us. The book was a game changer. It took no effort to give them those five copies and it created instant advocacy. And it gave the new HR person enough confidence in me, a perfect stranger, to be able to say to those trustees, "We need to be talking to this 401(k) person at Epstein Financial."

## TOP TEN BENEFITS OF
## WRITING A BOOK

Your book…

1. Will help you build the authority, celebrity, and expertise in your marketplace

2. Becomes your new business card: give your prospects your contact information and unique selling propositions with your book

3. Will foster dedication and passion … and turn your clients into fans

4. Will increase your visibility, credibility, and clout

5. Will increase the quantity and quality of referrals to your company

6. Can be used to get the coverage and free publicity you've always dreamed of

7. Can be used to leverage marketing dollars, reach more prospects, and get a better ROI on your marketing and sales efforts

8. Will help you harness your celebrity
   power to build your business

9. Can be used to create new connections and
   revenue streams and to find new business
   partners, joint ventures, and opportunities

10. Will create motivated customers who buy
    your services and reduce competition.
    It will create a brand in your market
    that people will recognize and value,
    and they will want to pay for your
    services over your competition.

## YOUR MEDIA PASS

The ACE formula I mentioned earlier is also
something that the media is always on the look-
out for when it comes to finding guest commen-
tators, both for visual media and the written word.
They could talk with just any financial advisor, of
course, but it looks so much better and lends so
much more credibility to their report when they
can state that the information provided comes

from an author with expertise in that field, such as, "Financial Advisor Charlie Epstein, author of *Paychecks for Life*."

I had a great instance of the ACE formula in action one day as I was walking to my local Starbucks. Standing just outside of the building was a local news anchor and her cameraman, and as I walked out she asked if she could interview me. The story she was working on actually had nothing to do with the financial industry, but I gave my statement and went on my way. After I left. however, it occurred to me that I'd missed a great opportunity. I should have given her a copy of my book!

I turned around and headed back only to see that they'd already left. However, the news van was still there and I could see them packing their equipment in, so I walked over and introduced myself again while also handing her a copy of my book.

"If you're ever looking for experts in the financial industry, here's my card and a copy of the book I wrote," I said.

Surprised, she took the book and replied that they were actually working on a story next week concerning 401(k)s. A week later, I got a phone call from the station asking me to be a guest commentator.

If I'd handed her my card and brochure, she probably would have forgotten me before I'd finished shaking her hand. But because of the book, I got free advertising on the local news.

## MAKING REFERRAL MARKETING EASY

Referral marketing is incredibly valuable because people are predisposed to believe you when their friends refer you to them. But here's the rub: how many financial advisors actually ask for referrals?

I've been coaching for close to fifteen years now and I'd say at least eighty percent of the advisors I work with fail to ask for a referral. Why? Because it makes them uncomfortable and/or they don't have a system for it. That's where the magic of being an author kicks in, because it makes getting referrals as fun and easy as handing out candy. People may not want a brochure, but they're excited to get a copy of a book.

Here are a few facts about referrals that you may already be familiar with:

- Twenty percent of your client base won't give you a referral no matter what.

- Sixty percent will give you a referral if asked, but they won't naturally do it—you have to encourage it.

- The last 20 percent will freely refer you because they're so excited to work with you.

So the big question is, how do you get that 60 percent to refer you?

By making it fun and easy to do so. If your clients that fall in that 60 percent range are excited about sharing something with their friends—such as a book that they found useful—then they'll refer you all day and all night. Giving a book away doesn't feel like selling, it feels like giving someone you care about something of value.

Taking it one step further, you could make the referral process even easier by using what I often refer to as the Trifecta system.

In essence, the Trifecta system is a simple way to get direct referrals from your clients without asking them to do anything more than sign a book.

## TRIFECTA SYSTEM

Step 1: Create a wish list of top one hundred businesses that you'd like to acquire as clients in the next one to three years.

Step 2: the next time you meet with a client, ask them if they would be willing to look at that list and tell you if they know anyone on it. Chances are that they know at least one or two them, maybe because they go to the same church or play racquetball together.

Step 3: Once they've identified an acquaintance, ask them if they would be willing to write a note to that person in the front of your book, recommending you as someone who's been of value to them. Then mail the book directly to that prospective client.

In three steps, you've created a powerful referral without burdening your client at all, and you're being proactive. It's a win-win system and about as painless as it gets.

## SPEAKING ENGAGEMENTS

Have you ever spoken for a fee? How about for free? Have you ever been invited to speak in front of a group about what you do for a living?

Speaking, hands down, is one of the best ways to acquire new clients for your business. Over a lifetime, one new client could be worth $100,000 or more to a financial advisor, so whether you're invited to speak for a fee or even for free at an event with your target audience, there will be at least a few people—if not a line of people—waiting to speak with you when you come off that stage.

Think, for instance, about how many nonprofit organizations are within an hour radius of your office. There are more than you think! Associations, chambers, Rotary Clubs—take some time to identify all of them. Each of these organizations are hungry for speakers and would likely be excited to hear from you – especially if you're the author of a book.

At Epstein Financial, we look to speak in front of those organizations that have something to do with our firm's two big niche markets: manufacturers and medical professionals. Once we've identified those groups, we send the person in charge of booking speakers a copy of the book and perhaps a link to a video showing why we would be a good speaker for their group.

If you do this, and if they like you, then the next question they'll likely have is, "What is your fee?"

Stop for a moment before giving them an answer to this one, because you have a choice here.

You could give them your fee and walk away with a few extra bucks in your pocket, or you could offer to speak for a reduced price—or for free—with the condition that the organization purchase a copy of your book for each of its members.

Now, what have you just done? You're getting a tacit endorsement from that organization because they not only thought you were important enough to speak to their members but they also approved of your book enough to buy copies of it for all of their members.

Case in point, I spoke at our local family business center on the topic of my second book, *Save America, Save: The Secrets of a Successful 401(k) Plan*. Before I got on stage, the center director walked up in front of about a hundred family business owners, all with businesses in our backyard, and said, "We're delighted to have one of our sponsors speaking tonight on his second book, *Save America, Save*. If you'd like to read it, Charlie has graciously given us several free copies, which are available in the back after his talk."

Of those in attendance, only about 50 percent came back for a copy of the book, but of those, ten of them are now clients. In fact, one of the business owners I gained from that meeting told me that he became a client because after that meeting he read the book and liked it enough to take the conversation further. That one client, who was worth $20,000 just to get started, was pre-sold all because of that one speaking event.

In fact, because of that one speaking engagement, my firm has indirectly made almost $100,000 just from the fees derived from those new 401(k) clients, and who knows where it will go from there.

It's not what you get paid up front for speaking or for selling one book—it's what you get paid over the lifetime of a client relationship that brings in the real money.

## DERIVATIVE MEDIA

Writing a book doesn't have to stop with just the book and using it to establish your own ACE formula. It's also an asset with multiple potential opportunities. A solid book can also be used to create:

- e-books
- audiobooks

- home study kits

- teleseminars

- webinars

- speeches

- boot camps

- seminars

Webinars, for instance, can be used to promote your business, but they can also be a resource for bringing in referral and strategic partners as guest speakers, who will then promote your webinar to their clients because they appeared on it. For financial advisors, these could be the local accounting firm you work with or the property and casualty firm or the law firms that you work with. Expanding on that idea, you could also reach out to the third-party administrator you bring business to or the recordkeepers or wholesalers you've worked with. Your potential list of guests is much longer than you may think.

And putting together a webinar is much more simple than you may think. Essentially, a webinar or teleseminar can be done in a conference room with a single camera. Record one of these once a quarter with different partners and you're building up a solid network of powerful promoters.

Take working with an accounting firm, for instance. If you aren't already working with one, find one with an audit department that audits 401(k) plans. Send them a copy of the book, introduce yourself as the author, and tell them how you'd love to do some collaborative marketing with a teleseminar where you could talk about the book and they could talk about audits. Our firm is doing that right now with an accounting firm and we're already talking about setting up a series of teleseminars.

You can also exponentially build your webinar traffic by enticing viewers with the offer of an autographed copy of your book for watching. It's hard to get these clients through the door right off the street, but by offering a teleseminar and a free book, you're building that viewership and potential client base. It's hard to turn down quick, free, useful information—that's the essence of powerful marketing.

## AUTHORITY NOW

After more than thirty-five years in the financial industry, I tell people that my biggest job now is getting people to spend their money on what they love to do. That's mainly what my books are about—they're about changing people's mind-set and getting them to think about their retirement not as the end of a journey but as the beginning of the time where they get to do the things they've always wanted to do. That's why I call them your "desirement years." In *Paychecks for Life*, I explain how you, the individual, can do this, and in *Save America, Save*, I share how you, the employer, can help your employees take full advantage of their desirement years. These books have helped me grow my business, focus on the part of the financial industry that I enjoy working in the most, and have been the foundation on which I've built my authority to the point where I'm being asked to appear on national television programs, such as Fox Business with Liz Claman.

I'm a living example of how becoming an author is truly the ultimate unfair advantage.

## NEXT STEPS

Charlie didn't become famous in his field and famous in his community overnight. It took years of strategically positioned steps to slowly, deliberately raise his profile. But today he commands the business and income he wants, and he's immensely happy doing it.

So how do you become a Charlie Epstein? How do you become slightly famous?

You build an Authority Marketing plan, something we actually call an Authority Marketing Blueprint, utilizing the Seven Pillars mentioned in this book. You then launch your plan and systematically implement that plan over time to build your authority. This is what we do day in and day out for financial professionals around the globe who are now authorities and leaders of their field.

We hope this book has left you enlightened and encouraged to deliberately use Authority Marketing to grow your own practice and position yourself as an expert and leader. Reading this was the first step. Whether you take the next steps depends on how much you truly want to succeed.

How does your authority rank? Take our Authority Assessment and see how you stack up against your competition.

www.forbesbooks.com/authority-assessment

# ABOUT THE AUTHORS

**Harper Tucker** is Chair of the Finance Practice at ForbesBooks. He empowers financial and legal innovators to enhance their industry influence and legacy through Authority Positioning. He actively brings in top thought leaders as authors, speakers, and brand authorities.

Harper and his team have worked with over one hundred and fifty financial and legal thought leaders to build their authority and personal brands, thus establishing him as an expert in these spaces. In today's world, clients seek advisors, CPAs, attorneys, and investment professionals they can trust. Harper is committed to guiding these professionals in communicating their credibility and expertise to current and potential clients through a published book and other Authority Positioning tactics.

From a young age, Harper has been fascinated with the financial and entrepreneurial world. Motivated by his educational pursuits at Clemson University, he worked tirelessly as a day trader while attending school full-time to completely fund his tuition. He actively applied the skills he learned within the classroom to the real-world, learning many lessons along the way. His experiences informed his financial knowledge and expertise early on.

Prior to joining the Advantage|ForbesBooks Team, Harper gained experience in business development and sales management with Cintas Corporation, where he served as one of the youngest sales managers in company history. His experiences demonstrate his unique ability to build trusting relationships and understand the end goal. Harper's tenure building such relationships translates into authority positioning and business growth opportunities for his clients. He received top marketing and leadership training through a two-year world renowned management trainee program. Over the past several years, Harper has also consulted with advisors in the financial industry. Harper's experiences serve him well in helping other professionals discover opportunities for growth.

In his free time, you can find Harper enjoying all that Charleston, South Carolina has to offer with his wife and son, Layne.

Harper Tucker
c/o ForbesBooks
65 Gadsden Street
Charleston, SC 29401
htucker@forbesbooks.com
843.518.6780

**Adam Witty** is the Chief Executive Officer of Advantage Media Group and ForbesBooks. Witty has built Advantage Media Group, The Business Growth Company™, into one of the largest business book publishers in America, serving over one thousand Members in forty states and thirteen countries. Advantage is a Five-Time Honoree on the Inc. 5000 list of America's most rapidly growing private companies in 2017, 2016, 2014, 2013, and 2012, and was named to the *Best Places to Work in South Carolina* list for 2013, 2014, and 2015.

Most recently, Advantage has partnered with Forbes to create ForbesBooks, the first book-publishing imprint for the global media company. Launched in 2016, ForbesBooks is the next step in Forbes' 100-year history of distribution and innovation in the media business. Utilizing the Forbes multi-platform media network, ForbesBooks offers a branding, visibility, and marketing platform to business authors. The exclusive imprint not only gets books to market faster than other top business book publishers, it also provides a holistic branding, visibility, and marketing platform for leading business leaders and idea makers.

In addition to his work with Advantage and Forbes-Books, Witty is a sought-after speaker, teacher, and consultant on marketing and business growth techniques for entrepreneurs and authors. He has shared the stage with Steve Forbes, Gene Simmons of KISS, Peter Guber, and Bobby Bowden. Witty has been featured in *The Wall Street Journal*, *Investor's Business Daily*, *USA Today*, and more.

He was named to Young Presidents' Organization 40 Under 40, 50 Most Progressive, and was named to the 2011 *Inc.* magazine 30 Under 30 list of "America's coolest entrepreneurs." In 2012, Witty was selected by the Chilean government to judge the prestigious Start-up Chile! entrepreneurship competition.

Witty is chairman of the not-for-profit Youth Entrepreneurship South Carolina, where they teach entrepreneurial skills to at-risk youth in every South Carolina public school. He also chairs the Clemson University's Spiro Entrepreneurship Institute board and sits on the College of Charleston Entrepreneurship Center board. Witty is an Eagle Scout, 2012 Clemson University Young Alumnus of the Year, a member of Young Presidents Organization (YPO), a member of Entrepreneurs' Organization (EO), Learning Officer for Digital Marketing and Media Board, and is happy to call Charleston, South Carolina home.